D0821890

Jane Goodall

Published in the United States of America by Cherry Lake Publishing
Ann Arbor, Michigan
www.cherrylakepublishing.com

Content Adviser: Ryan Emery Hughes, Doctoral Student, School of Education, University of Michigan
Reading Adviser: Marla Conn MS, Ed., Literacy specialist, Read-Ability, Inc.
Book Design: Jennifer Wahi
Illustrator: Jeff Bane

Photo Credits: © niepo/Shutterstock, 5; © S. Cooper Digital/Shutterstock, 7; © Kasza/Shutterstock, 9, 22; © Kjersti Joergenson/Shutterstock, 11; © Bettmann/CORBIS, 13, 23; © Everett Collection/Alamy, 15; © BRUCE COLEMAN INC. / Alamy Stock Photo, 17; © Penelope Breese/Liaison/Getty Images, 19; © EdStock/istock, 21; Cover, 8, 14, 18, Jeff Bane; Various frames throughout, Shutterstock Images

Library of Congress Cataloging-in-Publication Data

Names: Haldy, Emma E., author.
Title: Jane Goodall / Emma E. Haldy.
Description: Ann Arbor, Michigan : Cherry Lake Publishing, 2016. | Series: My itty-bitty bio | Includes bibliographical references and index.
Identifiers: LCCN 2015045149| ISBN 9781634710220 (hardcover) | ISBN 9781634712200 (pbk.) | ISBN 9781634711210 (pdf) | ISBN 9781634713191 (ebook)
Subjects: LCSH: Goodall, Jane, 1934---Juvenile literature. | Women primatologists--England--Biography--Juvenile literature. | Primatologists--England--Biography--Juvenile literature.
Classification: LCC QL31.G58 H35 2016 | DDC 590.92--dc23
LC record available at http://lccn.loc.gov/2015045149

Printed in the United States of America
Corporate Graphics

About the author: Emma E. Haldy is a former librarian and a proud Michigander. She lives with her husband, Joe, and an ever-growing collection of books.

About the illustrator: Jeff Bane and his two business partners own a studio along the American River in Folsom, California, home of the 1849 Gold Rush. When Jeff's not sketching or illustrating for clients, he's either swimming or kayaking in the river to relax.

I was born in London.
It was 1934.

I lived with my parents.
I had one sister.

I loved nature. I spent my free time outside.

I enjoyed learning about animals. I took notes. I drew sketches.

What is your favorite animal?

I wanted to visit Africa.
I worked. I saved my money.
I left on my trip.

I was excited to learn about African animals. I met a **researcher**. His name was Louis Leakey.

He wanted to learn about chimpanzees. He thought I could I help.

I went to their **habitat**. I watched the chimpanzees.

At first, they were scared of me. They ran away. I slowly earned their trust.

How would you get an
animal to trust you?

I became close to them.
I named them. I studied them.

I spent many years with them.
I made many **discoveries**.

They eat meat and vegetables. They make tools. They have **relationships**.

They are like people!

I wanted to share what I had learned.

I wrote books. People filmed my work. I became famous.

Today, I travel the world. I tell people about the chimpanzees.

I teach people about nature. I protect animals. I am proud to help the earth and all its creatures.

What would you like to ask me?

1957

1930

Born
1934

1960

2030

glossary

discoveries (dis-KUHV-er-eez) things that have been found or learned

habitat (HAB-i-tat) the place where a plant or animal is usually found

relationships (ri-LAY-shuhn-ships) the ways in which things or people are connected

researcher (REE-surch-er) someone who collects information

index